WHAT ON EARTH DO YOU DO

When Someone Dies?

second edition

Trevor Romain
illustrated by **Gabby Grant**

Library of Congress Cataloging-in-Publication Data
Names: Romain, Trevor, author. | Grant, Gabby, illustrator.
Title: What on earth do you do when someone dies? / Trevor Romain ; illustrated by Gabby Grant.
Description: 2nd edition. | Minneapolis, MN : Free Spirit Publishing, [2023] | Includes bibliographical references and index. | Audience: Ages 5–10
Identifiers: LCCN 2022052669 (print) | LCCN 2022052670 (ebook) | ISBN 9798765922569 (paperback) | ISBN 9798765922576 (ebook) | ISBN 9798765922583 (epub)
Subjects: LCSH: Grief in children—Juvenile literature. | Bereavement in children—Juvenile literature. | Adjustment (Psychology) in children—Juvenile literature. | BISAC: JUVENILE NONFICTION / Social Topics / Death, Grief, Bereavement | JUVENILE NONFICTION / Social Topics / Depression & Mental Illness
Classification: LCC BF723.G75 R65 2023 (print) | LCC BF723.G75 (ebook) | DDC 155.4/124—dc23/ eng/20230222
LC record available at https://lccn.loc.gov/2022052669
LC ebook record available at https://lccn.loc.gov/2022052670

Free Spirit Publishing does not have control over or assume responsibility for author or third-party websites and their content. At the time of this book's publication, all publications, organizations, websites, and other resources exist as described in this book; and all have been verified as of November 2022. Parents, teachers, and other adults: We strongly urge you to monitor children's use of the internet.

Edited by Alison Behnke and Elizabeth Verdick
Cover and interior design by Colleen Pidel
Illustrated by Gabby Grant

Printed by: 70548
Printed in: China
PO#: 9193

Free Spirit Publishing
An imprint of Teacher Created Materials
9850 51st Avenue North, Suite 100
Minneapolis, MN 55442
(612) 338-2068
help4kids@freespirit.com
freespirit.com

*I would like to thank the following experts
who read my book and helped me understand
how children cope with grief:*

William C. Kroen, Ph.D., LMHC

Thomas S. Greenspon, Ph.D., Licensed Psychologist

Harry Rauch, M.D., Child and Adolescent Psychiatrist

Debi Sharp, LSW

*I greatly appreciated your helpful comments
and feedback.*

CONTENTS

INTRODUCTION

Talking about death can be difficult and sometimes very upsetting. Lots of people don't like to talk about death. That can make it hard to share our feelings when we lose a loved one, a close friend, a pet, or someone we admire.

At the same time, we all hear a lot about death on the news because of illness, natural disasters, war, terrorism, crime, and other terrible events.

I wrote this book, and then updated it, because I know how hard it can be for people to deal with their feelings when they are grieving. In the book I share ideas, suggestions, thoughts, and tips to help anyone who is going through a tough time after experiencing a loss, like I did when my father passed away suddenly.

When I found out my dad had died, I was so shocked that all I could say was . . . *wow*. I couldn't sleep. My stomach hurt, and I didn't want to eat. The whole world seemed different to me. When someone you love dies, it's normal to feel shocked, sad, confused, worried, scared, or a lot of other painful feelings.

I decided to write this book in honor of my dad, who taught me to write and draw and care about other people. After his death, writing in my journal helped me sort out my feelings and remember all the ways my dad was special. It gave me a way to feel more peaceful inside.

Most importantly, I wrote this book for you. If you've lost someone you care about, I hope this book answers the questions you have. I hope it gives you the words and strength you need during this painful time in your life. And I hope you believe me when I say that you won't always feel as sad and hurt and confused as you do now. You will feel better—maybe not right away, but in the coming weeks or months, *you will feel better.*

Trevor Romain

WHY DO PEOPLE HAVE TO DIE?

When we're born, we experience life. When our life ends, we experience death. Death happens to all living things on Earth.

Some people die when they're really old. Others die when they get very, very sick with an illness like cancer, heart disease, or COVID-19. Still others die from being badly hurt in accidents or natural disasters, or because of shootings or other violence. No matter how someone dies, family and friends of that person feel sad and upset.

My 14-year-old friend Vicki, who had cancer, was very wise. One time, we were talking about dying, and she told me something important. She said that people don't talk about death very often, which makes it harder to understand. And when we don't understand something, we're more likely to be afraid of it. Instead of being scared, talk to someone you love about what's on your mind.

Sometimes adults don't want to scare kids by talking about death, and that can leave kids feeling lonely and empty. If you want to talk about what you are experiencing, let adults know that it would help you to talk about your thoughts, feelings, and questions. It's also okay to tell someone you don't feel like talking at that moment if you would prefer not to.

AM I GOING TO DIE TOO?

If someone close to you has died, you might be afraid that you're going to die. It may help to know that most people live for a long, long time, and you probably will too.

You may also wonder if other people you love or care about are going to die. It's natural to worry like this. These kinds of fears might even keep you awake all night.

It's kind of like worrying about a monster in your closet. It can be scarier to lie in bed alone thinking about the monster than it is to open the closet and see what's really there. The best way to deal with something you're afraid of is to face it. How? Talk about it. Let somebody know that you feel frightened.

WHO CAN I TALK TO?

The adults in your life may be so upset about the death that they forget to talk to you about how you're doing. But the more you discuss the death, the less scary it becomes. If you're wondering who you can talk to, here are some ideas:

- a parent or another family member
- a neighbor or friend of the family
- someone at your place of worship, if you go to one
- your teacher or principal
- a counselor or youth group leader

WHAT IS IT LIKE TO DIE?

No one alive knows exactly what it's like to die. When people die, their minds, bodies, and brains stop working. They can't think, move, feel, hear, or breathe. They can't tell anyone else what death is like.

You might have heard stories about people who almost died. Some of them believe they saw things (like a bright light) or heard things (like the voices of people they knew who had already died). But no one who is alive can know for sure what it is like to die.

I like to believe that death is calm and peaceful. I was with my young friend René when she died, and I saw her smile right before she passed away. I'll never forget her peaceful smile.

WHY AM I HURTING SO MUCH?

When someone you love dies, your feelings get all stirred up. You may be full of tears, anger, worry, and hurt. You might feel so sad and upset that you want to curl up in a ball and hide. This is because you're experiencing grief. Grief is the deepest sadness a person can feel.

It helps to be able to name and describe all of your feelings.
Ask yourself how you feel right now. Are you:

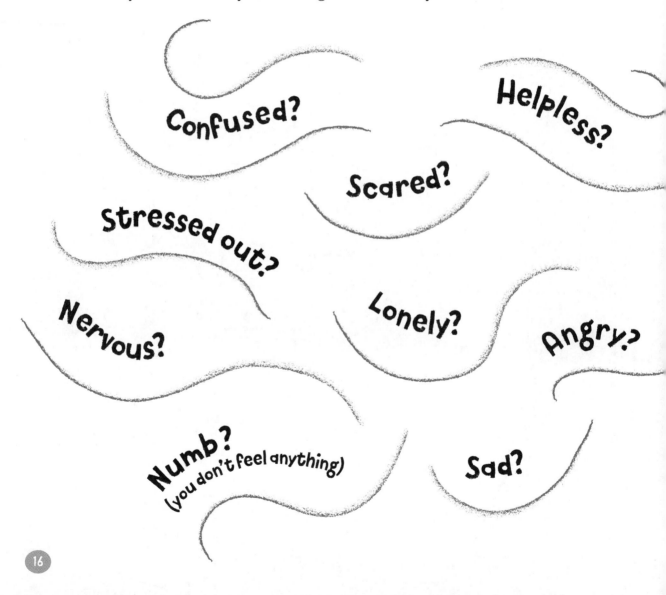

Confused?

Helpless?

Scared?

Stressed out?

Lonely?

Nervous?

Angry?

Numb?
(you don't feel anything)

Sad?

If none of these words fit your feelings, think of some words that do. You can write the words and draw how you feel. Or you can even make up your own words. When I was a kid, my family made up words for things. Like the word *badsad*. We used that when we were really sad. Or the word *skadoodled*, which we used when we found it hard to concentrate and our minds fclt like they were filled with sketch doodles.

When you're hurting deeply inside, you may not feel like eating. You may have bad dreams or trouble sleeping at night. You may even find yourself searching for the person who died (though you know they aren't coming back). And you may be hoping, wishing, or praying to see them again.

Your mind and body are working very hard to deal with what has happened.

IS IT OKAY TO CRY?

Sometimes people who have lost a loved one try to pretend the death didn't happen. Or they act like they aren't hurting as much as they really are. Either way, they keep their feelings locked inside.

If you're keeping your feelings locked up, it's like building a huge wall around yourself—a wall that no one can climb over. What can you do to break down this wall? You can cry.

Crying is okay. You don't have to hide your feelings or put
on a brave face. No matter what anyone might say, you aren't
a baby or weak if you cry. Crying helps you set your feelings
free. It can let others know you need some help. And it helps
you feel your sadness, move through it, and start to feel a little
better—bit by bit.

IS THE DEATH MY FAULT?

One question many kids ask is, "Was it my fault the person died?" They wonder things like: "Was it because I was bad?" "Did this happen because I didn't say my prayers?" "Could I have done something to stop the death from happening?"

If you're having these thoughts, you're feeling guilty. You're blaming yourself for the death. But you shouldn't. Here's something you need to understand: *If someone you love dies, it's not your fault.*

Sometimes, when kids know that someone is dying or has died, they have a dream about the person. In the dream, they may see the person die, and they believe it's *their* fault it happened. Have you had this kind of dream? If you have, you need to know that your dream didn't cause the death.

This is really important, so I'll say it one more time: *If someone you love dies, it's NOT your fault.*

Dreams can't make someone die. Neither can thinking bad thoughts, telling a lie, or misbehaving.

WHAT IF I JUST WANT TO BE ALONE?

After my dad died, there was a brief time when I wanted to be left alone. I didn't know what to feel, say, or do. I trembled a lot and walked around in a daze. It was like a bad dream.

I didn't want anyone to hug me or hold me. People wanted to comfort me, but I pushed them away. You might feel like this yourself. Maybe you don't want people to know how sad you are. Or maybe you're too upset to talk.

Part of you may wish everyone would just go away.
But another part of you, deep down inside,
probably needs people more than ever.
Let your family and friends help you.
You can help them too.

Sometimes it's fine to be alone. You may want to sit and think about the person who died. You might want to cry without anyone else around. All of that is okay. It's perfectly normal to have alone time when you're grieving.

But being on your own *too* much can make you feel lonely and empty inside. If you want to spend time alone, but feel lonely when you do, try to find a balance. Or find something in-between. You could be in a room with other people and create a special place there, just for yourself. That way you can feel alone, but not lonely, because you know that people who love you are right there if you need them. When I was little, I used to make a little fort out of couch pillows. I'd crawl inside when I wanted to be alone but didn't want to be by myself.

WHAT CAN I DO IF I'M ANGRY?

Some kids feel angry after the death of a loved one. They say, "This is so unfair!" Or, "Why did this have to happen to me!?" They're mad about what they've lost, and missing the person makes them even madder.

If you feel this way, you might yell at people you love or say things to hurt them. You might take out your anger on your friends or your pet, even though you don't mean to.

Instead, you can learn to handle your anger in other ways. When you get mad, try one of these ideas:

- Talk to someone about your feelings.
- Hit your pillow or your mattress with your fists.
- Go to a field or park and yell.
- Run, throw a ball, or swim.

- Take your dog for a long walk.
- Pound and squash a piece of clay as hard as you want.
- Pretend your anger is a piece of paper and rip it into shreds or little pieces.
- Pop bubble wrap.
- Breathe slowly and deeply.
- Run warm water over your hands and pretend you're rinsing off your anger.
- Ask an adult you trust to help you do something kind for someone else.

WILL I EVER FEEL BETTER?

Feelings like sadness, anger, and worry will probably hit you in waves. One moment, you'll feel better. And the next, you'll feel worse than ever. Your emotions may go up and down like a roller coaster.

Maybe you're wishing you had a magic formula that would take away the pain you're feeling right away. Unfortunately, there isn't one. But here are three good things you can do to help yourself.

1. *Be active.* Go outdoors, run around, and shout out loud.

2. *Show your feelings.* Cry if you need to, and talk to your family or friends. When you hurt a lot, be sure to get a hug from someone you love. Or give your pet a hug.

3. *Keep a journal about your feelings.* A journal is a place for writing and drawing your private thoughts.

If you like the idea of keeping a journal, you can use a notebook or sketchbook. Or you can use a computer or tablet. Whatever you choose, this will be your special place to write or draw how you feel.

Use this journal for as long as you need to. Work on it alone or with others. You can share your art and writing, if you want. Or you can keep it to yourself.

IS IT STILL OKAY TO HAVE FUN?

Here's something my seven-year-old friend Audrey told me before she died: "Having fun is a good way to forget about things that make you sad." Even though someone you love has died, it's all right for you to still smile and laugh and enjoy life. It doesn't mean you don't remember or miss the person who died. And it doesn't mean you don't still feel sad sometimes too.

Most people agree that the person who died would *want* you to go on with your life. It's healthy for you to stay busy and spend time doing the things you normally like to do, such as playing and talking to your friends. It may help to keep a list of things that make you smile—a Smile List! You can look at it whenever you need cheering up. This can help make the hurt not hurt so much.

WHERE HAS THE PERSON GONE?

One of the hardest things to understand is what happens after people die. Where do they go? Are they in heaven? Are they spirits or ghosts?

People have many different ideas about what happens after death. These ideas can be related to people's religion (if they are part of one), their culture, their traditions, and their personal beliefs. If you're not sure what to think or what you believe, that's okay. Talk to your family about your questions.

WHAT HAPPENS TO THE PERSON'S BODY?

People take care of their loved ones who have died in different ways. In many cultures, washing and dressing the person who died is very important. After the body has been prepared in a special way, it may be placed in a coffin or casket. These are boxes or chests to bury someone in.

Some people prefer having a natural burial after they die. Sometimes this is also called a green burial. This means that instead of being in a coffin, they are wrapped in a special cloth and placed in a grave. (This is actually how people were buried for thousands of years, before coffins were invented.) Some people have seeds placed in the cloth so pretty flowers, or even trees, grow above where they are laid to rest.

Many kids are curious about what a dead body looks like. They wonder if it will be scary or gross. After the body is prepared for burial, the person who died usually looks calm and peaceful. The eyes and mouth will be closed, as if the person were asleep.

Another method of taking care of the body is a process called cremation. This means the body is burned in very high heat. After cremation, only ashes remain.

Being burned or buried may sound terrible, but the person who died can't feel these things when they happen.

If the person who died is cremated, the family might keep the ashes in a vase known as an urn, or in a special handmade box, or in a container that means something to the family. Some families keep this container in a special place. Others bury the ashes in the ground or scatter them somewhere that the person loved.

For example, my friend Howard loved a mountain close to where he lived. When he died, his parents went to the top of the mountain and scattered Howard's ashes into the wind.

The next spring, pretty flowers bloomed along the mountainside. Howard's parents said that his colorful spirit was captured in each and every flower.

HOW DO WE HONOR THE PERSON WHO DIED?

Most families and communities have special ways to honor someone who has died. They may wear certain colors like black or white as a sign of respect. Some families pray, some dance, some light candles, and some hold a feast. Others cover all the paintings and mirrors in their home. Or they might burn incense or paper goods. These traditions and many others have been passed down in families and cultures for years and years.

Some families hold a ceremony known as a viewing or a visitation, where families "watch over" the dead, or look at the person one last time. (Sometimes this is called a *wake*, which can be confusing. It doesn't mean the person is "awake" or will "wake up.")

If you feel nervous about seeing the body of the person who died, that's natural. But you still might get comfort from saying goodbye to the person in this way. If you feel unsure or if you have questions, talk to an adult you trust.

WHAT IS A FUNERAL OR MEMORIAL SERVICE?

Some families hold a ceremony called a funeral. This often takes place in a place of worship or in a building called a funeral home. Another kind of ceremony is a memorial service, which may be held in a house of worship or in some other place that was special to the person who died.

At these services, family and friends talk about their loved one, sing, pray, or play music. This is how they mourn the loss of the person, or express their grief.

Funerals, memorial services, and other ceremonies like this are important. They can help us heal after someone we love dies. But your parents or other adults might not be sure if you want to go. They might also be feeling their own grief and forget to ask you what you really want.

If you do want to go to the service, talk to your family about it. And if you don't go, you can still mourn your loved one in your own special way:

- Make a hand-drawn card.
- Think about the person who died.
- Write your favorite memory or a story about them.
- Gather things the person gave you (like letters or gifts) and spend time looking at and touching them.
- Say out loud "I love you and miss you."

Many people, including members of your family, will be sad on the day of the funeral or memorial service. Sometimes it's hard for kids to see adults cry. Remember that crying sets feelings free—for anyone, no matter what age they are.

The service might make you feel like crying and smiling at the same time. You may miss the person who died, but also think about the good times you had together. Feeling this mixture of emotions is very common and totally normal.

Whether you feel sad or comforted (or both), you can show it by giving hugs or holding hands with other people who are there. (My six-year-old friend Alex told me that the best thing you can do for someone who is really sad is hold their hand.)

After the ceremony, the body of the person who died may be taken away. After that, depending on the person's culture, family, and where they live, many different things might happen.

In some places, the body goes into a car called a hearse. Then it goes to a cemetery, a place where the body is laid to rest. Here the coffin or casket is placed in a grave, which could be a hole in the ground or a space in a special building. The grave may later be marked with a special memorial called a headstone.

If you've seen a cemetery in a scary movie, you may think it's an awful place to go. Many movies show frightening cemeteries that are dark and filled with ghosts. Actually, most cemeteries aren't scary. They're quiet and peaceful. They can even be beautiful.

You won't see ghosts, but you will see graves, headstones, and lots of flowers. (Many people bring flowers to honor their dead.)

HOW CAN I SAY GOODBYE?

There are many ways to say goodbye to someone who dies. If the person is buried at a cemetery, you can visit the grave and say goodbye out loud. Or you can just say it softly to yourself—wherever you are. You can write a goodbye letter or draw a goodbye picture. Do whatever helps you feel better and more peaceful inside.

I said goodbye to my dad by sitting by myself in his art studio and talking to him as if he were there. I told him that I would look after my mom and my brother and sister. I let him know that I'd never forget him.

I remember my dad each day by keeping a photo of him on my desk in my writing studio. When I look at his picture, I think of the happy times I had with him. Sometimes I just look at him and cry a little. Either way, I feel better afterward.

Here are some ways to remember someone who has died:

- Put photos of the person in a special album.
- Plant a tree or flower garden in memory of the person.
- Have a get-together with family and friends, so all of you can remember the good times.
- Ask your family to light a candle every year on the person's birthday.
- Tell your friends how special the person was to you.
- Dedicate a basketball, soccer, baseball, or other game in honor of the person.

- Donate money in the name of the person who died to a special organization that you care about, or that your loved one cared about. You could ask a supportive adult for help with this idea.

- Visit the place where the person is buried or where their ashes were scattered.

- Draw a picture of your loved one or write a poem in their honor. You can display it in your room, or place it on the grave or near where their ashes are kept.

- Put something that belonged to your loved one in a special place. Look at it when you're feeling sad or when you just want to remember them.

When someone you love dies, your life changes. If you've lost a parent, you may wonder who will take care of you now. If you've lost a sibling or close friend, your life may feel emptier.

These kinds of changes are hard to accept. If you're worried about your future, talk to an adult who will understand. Ask this person for advice (and a hug, if you need one).

It also helps to talk to your friends. They may be afraid to call you or invite you over because they know you're feeling sad. You can let them know that you still want to be friends. Tell them it's okay for them to talk to you about the death, and even ask you questions. Remind your friends that they don't have to treat you differently.

As time goes by, you'll begin to feel less worried, sad, angry, confused, and lonely. It may not seem possible, but it's true. Time helps heal the pain.

On birthdays, holidays, and other special days, memories of the person who died may come flooding back. You may be sad all over again. If you're grieving during these times, share your thoughts and memories. Let the people who love you know how you're feeling.

You may have lost someone special to you, but something will always remain—your memories. Hold tight to these memories by looking at your photos, keepsakes, drawings, or journal. Think about how much the person meant to you, and about all the fun times you shared. You may find it comforting to remember your loved one's smile, voice, or laugh.

There's one more very important thing you need to know:
Remembering can help someone live on forever . . . in your
mind and in your heart.

WHERE ELSE CAN I GO FOR HELP?

In the books listed here, you can find more information about coping with the death of a loved one and dealing with your grief. Ask a parent or other adult to take you to a local library or bookstore. Your school library can be a good resource too. Or ask an adult to help you look online for additional books, plus helpful websites, videos, podcasts, or even movies.

The Dead Bird by Margaret Wise Brown, illustrated by Christian Robinson (New York: HarperCollins, 2016). Originally published in 1938, this book tells the story of some children who find a dead bird, bury it, and say their goodbyes.

How I Feel: Grief Journal for Kids by Mia Roldan (Oakland, CA: Rockridge Press, 2022). This guided journal is filled with prompts and exercises to help you explore your emotions, find comfort and peace, and hold memories of your loved one close.

The Invisible String by Patrice Karst, illustrated by Joanne Lew-Vriethoff (New York: Little, Brown and Company, 2018). In this story, a mother tells her two children that they're all connected by an invisible string. Together they explore questions about the unbreakable connections between people, which last even after someone we love dies.

The Tenth Good Thing About Barney by Judith Viorst, illustrated by Erik Blegvad (New York: Atheneum, 1987). When Barney the cat dies, his young owner feels so sad that he can't do anything. His mother suggests that he write a list of ten good things about Barney, so the boy can think about all the good times they had.

Violet the Snowgirl: A Story of Loss and Healing by Lisa L. Walsh, illustrated by Wendy Leach (Minneapolis: Free Spirit Publishing, 2020). Jerzie, her little brother, Josiah, and their grandma spend a wonderful day outside building and playing with Violet, a snowgirl that becomes a pilot, a teacher, a vet, and even their late granddad throughout the day. But when a warm day comes and Violet melts, Jerzie has to find ways to cope with her grief.

What Does Grief Feel Like? by Korie Leigh, illustrated by Mike Malbrough (Minneapolis: Free Spirit Publishing, 2023). This book talks about how, when a loved one dies, everyone's grief is a little different. It also asks you questions about how your grief feels.

When Someone Dies by Andrea Dorn (Eau Claire, WI: PESI Publishing, 2022). This book helps you use mindfulness to say goodbye to someone who has died, understand your feelings, and work through your grief.

ABOUT THE AUTHOR AND ILLUSTRATOR

Trevor Romain describes himself as a story farmer. He is an award-winning author and illustrator as well as a sought-after public speaker. His books have sold more than a million copies and been published in 22 languages. For more than 30 years, Trevor has traveled the world,  speaking to thousands of children. Trevor is well known for his work with the Make-A-Wish Foundation, the United Nations, UNICEF, the USO, and the Comfort Crew for Military Kids, which he cofounded. Trevor is a past board president of the American Childhood Cancer Organization. Trevor was born in South Africa but now resides on Kaua'i in Hawai'i.

Gabby Grant had a slightly wobbly path to illustration. She studied art history, then worked in administration and marketing until returning to the University of Westminster and getting another degree in illustration. That led to a fun spin through the world

of prop making for television and film. Since then, she's worked mainly in picture books and educational publishing. While she particularly likes drawing children, grumpy cats, crocodiles, dragons, guinea pigs, and octopi, she's happy as long as she's creating something. Gabby lives in London, England.